12 IMMUTABLE LAWS OF NEGOTIATION

(The Path to Success)

IYKE OFUEBO

TABLE OF CONTENTS

Preface

Introduction

Chapter 1.	What is Negotiation?
Chapter 2	The Law of Preparation
Chapter 3	The Law of Leverage
Chapter 4	The Law of Silence
Chapter 5	The Law of Flexibility
Chapter 6	The Law of Patience
Chapter 7	The Law of Reciprocity
Chapter 8	The Law of the Walkaway
Chapter 9	The Law of Emotional Control
Chapter 10	The Law of Framing
Chapter 11	The Law of Win-Win
Chapter 12	The Law of Persistence
Chapter 13	The Law of Value Perception
Chapter 14	Mastering the Laws
Final Note	

PREFACE

Negotiation is the quiet engine behind every success story. Whether you're an entrepreneur closing a multi-million dollar deal, a job seeker securing your dream position, or a parent finding common ground with your teenager, negotiation is at the heart of it all. Yet so many people shy away from it, seeing negotiation as a battleground filled with tension, compromise, and uncertainty. This book was written to change that perception.

As a negotiation specialist, I've spent years observing, learning, and teaching the art of negotiation. Through experience and countless interactions, I have realized that the most effective negotiators are not those who dominate the conversation or outmanoeuvre the other party. They are the ones who understand and apply timeless principles—principles that not only help them achieve their goals but also foster trust, collaboration, and long-term success.

The 12 Immutable Laws of Negotiation is more than just a collection of strategies; it's a roadmap to navigating the complexities of human interaction. It's about learning how to balance your interests with those of the other party, how to leverage power without abusing it, and how to walk away from the table stronger than when you sat down.

The laws outlined in this book aren't just theoretical concepts—they are actionable, practical tools that anyone can use. Whether you're an experienced professional or someone new to negotiation, these laws will equip you with the skills you need to approach any negotiation with confidence and clarity.

This book is for anyone who wants to harness the power of negotiation in their personal and professional lives. You don't need to be a corporate leader or a seasoned dealmaker to benefit from these insights. Negotiation touches every aspect of life, and the better you become at it, the more opportunities you'll unlock.

So as you dive into these pages, remember: negotiation isn't just about winning a deal. It's about creating value, building relationships, and driving progress. Each law you'll learn is a stepping stone toward mastering this critical life skill. With practice and dedication, these principles will become part of how you approach every conversation, every deal, and every opportunity.

Thank you for embarking on this journey with me. May this book transform the way you negotiate and open doors you never thought possible.

Let's begin…

INTRODUCTION

The 12 Immutable Laws of Negotiation are timeless principles designed to give you the strategic advantage in any negotiation setting. These laws are drawn from psychology, business, and personal development, and they are applicable whether you are negotiating a high-stakes business deal or resolving a personal conflict.

In this book, you'll learn:

How to prepare like a professional so that you walk into every negotiation with confidence.

How to leverage silence, emotion, and framing to influence outcomes in your favour.

How to build trust and reciprocity so that both parties leave the table satisfied and open to future collaboration.

How to walk away when the deal doesn't serve your best interests —knowing that the power to leave can be your greatest strength.

By the end of this book, you won't just understand negotiation —you'll be able to master it. You'll be able to see through the fog of uncertainty, manage emotional pressure, and emerge from negotiations with outcomes that benefit you both financially and strategically. These laws are your roadmap to navigating the complex dynamics of negotiation and transforming how you approach every deal in life.

Who Is This Book For?

This book is for anyone who wants to improve their ability to negotiate and achieve better results in both their personal and professional lives. Whether you're a seasoned business executive or someone who's just beginning to understand the art of negotiation, the principles outlined in these pages will offer valuable insights.

Business Leaders and Entrepreneurs: If you are running a business, managing a team, or negotiating with clients, mastering these laws will enable you to secure better deals, grow your company, and build stronger partnerships.

Employees and Job Seekers: For those negotiating salaries, promotions, or new opportunities, these laws will empower you to advocate for yourself with confidence, ensuring that you achieve the professional recognition and rewards you deserve.

Salespeople and Consultants: Negotiation is the cornerstone of your profession. This book will give you the tools to close deals more effectively, create long-term client relationships, and build your career on a foundation of successful outcomes.

Everyday Negotiators: Whether you're negotiating the price of a car, discussing finances with your partner, or making a significant purchase, the principles in this book will help you achieve the best possible outcome.

Negotiation is a Skill, Not a Gift

Many people believe that negotiation is an inherent talent—that some are born with the ability to persuade, influence, and close deals, while others simply aren't. This couldn't be further from the truth. Negotiation is a learned skill. It's something that can be studied, practiced, and mastered, just like any other discipline. And with the right tools and mindset, anyone can become an exceptional negotiator.

Throughout this book, we will explore the strategies and tactics that top negotiators use to consistently win. But more importantly, you will learn how to internalize these strategies so that they become second nature. With practice, these 12 laws will become part of your negotiation DNA, guiding your decisions and actions with instinctive precision.

Your Journey Begins Now

Every chapter of this book is designed to take you deeper into the heart of successful negotiation. Each law offers a new piece of the puzzle, building on the last to create a complete framework for mastering the negotiation process. You'll learn how to prepare effectively, read the other side, manage emotions, and use leverage to achieve the best possible outcomes.

But remember: knowledge alone won't make you a better negotiator. It's what you do with that knowledge that counts. As you read through these laws, make a commitment to practice them in your daily life. Test them out in small conversations and low-stakes negotiations. With time and experience, you'll develop the confidence and intuition to tackle even the most complex negotiations with ease.

By the time you finish this book, you'll be armed with the skills, mindset, and strategies to negotiate with confidence, clarity, and power. Your ability to influence outcomes and secure what you want in life will never be the same.

By mastering these 12 Immutable Laws of Negotiation, you will not only increase your success in negotiations but also transform the way you approach problem-solving, communication, and leadership. Your journey to becoming a master negotiator starts today.

So, are you ready to become a master negotiator? Let's begin.

CHAPTER 1

What is Negotiation?

Negotiation is a word that carries immense weight in both personal and professional realms. At its core, it's about reaching agreements, but it goes far deeper than simply getting a deal done. Scholars, business leaders, and professionals alike have offered countless definitions of negotiation, each highlighting different aspects of this critical skill.

Let's begin by exploring how others have defined negotiation, and then we'll arrive at the unique definition that serves as the foundation of this book.

Definitions by Others:

1. "Negotiation is the process of communicating back and forth for the purpose of reaching a joint decision."

– Roger Fisher and William Ury, "Getting to Yes"

Fisher and Ury, pioneers of negotiation theory, emphasize negotiation as a back-and-forth communication aimed at achieving a joint outcome. Their definition points to the collaborative aspect of negotiation, where both parties work toward a mutual decision.

2. "Negotiation is a strategic discussion that resolves an issue in a way that both parties find acceptable."

– Investopedia

This definition underlines the practical and strategic side of negotiation. It suggests that a successful negotiation isn't just about reaching any solution—it's about finding one that both sides can agree to, which often requires compromise and careful consideration of each party's needs.

3. "Negotiation is a basic means of getting what you want from others. It is back-and-forth communication designed to reach an agreement when you and the other side have some interests that are shared and others that are opposed."

– Herb Cohen, "You Can Negotiate Anything"

Herb Cohen frames negotiation as a fundamental way to achieve what you want by navigating both shared and opposing interests. His definition highlights the fact that negotiation often involves conflict but also the potential for alignment.

4. "Negotiation is the art of letting the other side have your way."

– Daniele Vare, Italian Diplomat

This wittier take on negotiation captures its persuasive nature. Vare's definition highlights the subtlety of negotiation, where true mastery involves getting the other party to willingly agree to your terms, often without realizing they've been persuaded.

5. "Negotiation is the use of information and power to affect behavior within a web of tension."

– John R. French and Bertram Raven, Social Psychologists

This perspective dives into the psychological aspects of negotiation, focusing on power dynamics and the strategic use of information. It suggests that negotiation is more than just conversation—it's a deliberate process that manages tensions between parties.

In one of my earlier works, I defined negotiation as "the art of using time and information to affect a tensed emotional network." This definition highlights the dual importance of patience and intelligence in navigating complex negotiations.

When emotions flare, people often make hasty decisions. As a negotiator, your ability to wait, manage the tension, and release information at the right moment can shift the dynamics of the conversation, giving you an edge over the other party.

Negotiation is not just about logic and reason; it often takes place in a network of emotions where tensions run high, especially when the stakes are significant. It's in these moments of pressure that the strategic use of time and information becomes a powerful tool.

The emotional network in any negotiation is like a web of interconnected feelings—anxiety, excitement, frustration, and anticipation. Your task is to recognize this web and manipulate its tension to your advantage. By holding back key information or releasing it strategically, and by controlling the flow of time—whether through pauses, delays, or urgent action—you can shape the emotional landscape of the negotiation.

While the above definitions capture important aspects of negotiation, this book approaches negotiation as a far more nuanced and strategic process. In The 12 Immutable Laws of Negotiation, we define negotiation as:

"Negotiation is the art and science of creating value through strategic communication, leveraging influence, and aligning mutual interests, while maintaining the flexibility to adapt, the patience to wait, and the power to walk away."

This definition combines the art of understanding human dynamics with the science of strategic thinking and preparation. It emphasizes that negotiation is not just about compromise or persuasion, but about creating value for all parties involved. Here's a breakdown of what makes this definition unique:

Creating Value: Negotiation is not just about winning or getting what you want; it is about creating outcomes that benefit everyone involved, leading to sustainable success.

Strategic Communication: The way you communicate—both verbally and non-verbally—is crucial. Negotiation is a carefully calculated process where timing, wording, and tone make all the difference.

Leveraging Influence: Influence is one of the most powerful tools in negotiation. Whether it's through silence, emotional intelligence, or framing the conversation, knowing how to sway the other party is key.

Aligning Mutual Interests: At its core, successful negotiation is about finding common ground. It's about aligning the interests of both parties in a way that feels beneficial for everyone.

Flexibility, Patience, and Power: The ability to adapt, wait for the right moment, and walk away when necessary are essential to maintaining control and ensuring the best possible outcome.

In essence, this book views negotiation as a dynamic, fluid process that requires careful balance, insight, and skill. It's about more than getting a deal—it's about creating win-win outcomes that stand the test of time, empowering you to lead with influence and succeed in any arena.

As you delve deeper into the 12 Immutable Laws of negotiation, remember that negotiation is not a rigid set of rules, but a fluid and evolving skill set. The tools and principles outlined in this book will allow you to approach any negotiation—whether in the boardroom, across the table from a client, or in your personal life—with confidence, clarity, and control.

Negotiation is your gateway to success. Now that you understand what it truly is, you are ready to master it.

Negotiation is everywhere. From the boardroom to the marketplace, from the hiring table to family discussions, negotiation is the thread that weaves through nearly every significant interaction in life. We negotiate our salaries, our contracts, our partnerships, and even the smaller day-to-day decisions, like where to eat or how to spend our weekends. Yet, despite its omnipresence, negotiation remains an elusive skill for many.

Why is that? Why do some people seem to glide effortlessly through negotiations, securing great deals and building strong relationships, while others feel uncertain, anxious, or even defeated by the process? The answer often lies in a misunderstanding of what negotiation truly is, and what it takes to be successful at it.

This book is about changing that. It's about turning negotiation from a mysterious, anxiety-inducing process into a powerful tool you can wield with confidence. Whether you're negotiating a million-dollar contract or simply working to get the best deal on a car, The 12 Immutable Laws of Negotiation will give you a framework that guarantees results.

Why Negotiation Matters Now More Than Ever

We live in an increasingly complex world where the ability to influence others, create value, and navigate conflict has never been more important. As the global marketplace becomes more competitive, the stakes in every negotiation rise. Being a skilled negotiator no longer gives you just an edge—it's a requirement for survival and success in many fields. Whether you're an entrepreneur, an executive, a freelancer, or someone looking to advance in your career, mastering negotiation is one of the most valuable skills you can develop.

Despite its importance, many people approach negotiation the wrong way. They think it's about domination or manipulation—winning at the expense of the other party. But true negotiation isn't about crushing your opponent; it's about finding the sweet spot where both parties feel they've gained something of value. It's about creating win-win scenarios, building relationships, and laying the foundation for long-term success.

CHAPTER 2

The Law of Preparation: Know Thy Battlefield

Before you enter any negotiation, preparation is your first weapon. Understanding the desires, motivations, and potential concessions of both parties is paramount. Research your opponent, study their needs, and arm yourself with all possible information. This is where battles are won or lost before the first word is spoken.

In negotiation, unpreparedness is a sin. Preparation is not just recommended; it is essential.

Preparation is your most powerful asset. The mistake most people make is rushing into discussions without a solid understanding of the terrain—this includes the people, stakes, and variables involved. Successful negotiators don't leave things to chance. They thoroughly research the other party's motivations, goals, and weaknesses. They analyse market conditions, trends, and possible alternatives.

Negotiation is a form of strategic warfare, and the first battle takes place before anyone even sits down at the table. Preparation isn't just about gathering information; it's about understanding the battlefield. Who are you negotiating with? What are their motivations, their pain points, their constraints? The negotiator who walks into a meeting blind has already lost half the battle.

Knowledge of Your Opponent: In every negotiation, understanding your opponent's needs, desires, and limitations gives you a crucial advantage. It's not just about knowing what they want, but why they want it. This allows you to tailor your proposals to their underlying motivations, which are often more flexible than their stated positions.

Scenario Planning: Before the negotiation begins, successful negotiators map out multiple possible scenarios. They anticipate objections, plan their responses, and prepare counteroffers. Think through "What if" scenarios: What if they say yes immediately? What if they reject my offer outright? What if they bring in a third party? Being prepared for every possible turn gives you the upper hand.

Actionable Takeaway:

Before entering any negotiation, create a detailed checklist: Who is the other party? What are their goals and challenges? What are your goals? What concessions are you willing to make? Preparation turns uncertainty into clarity.

- Gather as much information as possible about the other party.
- Understand their pain points and what they stand to gain or lose.
- Prepare scenarios and responses for different outcomes.

Application

a. A real estate investor will carefully and intentionally study the property, the seller's financial situation, and market trends before making an offer. Armed with this data, he will confidently present an offer that meets the seller's needs but secures them a profitable deal.

b. Imagine a job candidate preparing for a salary negotiation. They don't just look at average salary data; they research the company's financial health, study the competitive landscape, and even gauge how urgently the company needs to fill the position. By doing so, they gain the confidence to push for higher compensation, knowing the company has more flexibility than initially apparent.

CHAPTER 3

The Law of Leverage: Power Lies with Those Who Control Value

Negotiation is a game of leverage, and the one who controls the most value wins. To succeed, identify what you possess that the other party needs, and magnify its importance.

Leverage is the currency of negotiation. It is what separates success from failure. Leverage is not just about having something the other party wants—it's about understanding how critical your offering is to them. The party with the greatest leverage controls the negotiation. This can be financial resources, time, expertise or even relationships. Knowing your leverage and using it wisely is the key to tipping the scales in your favour. However, leverage can also be hidden—something that may not seem valuable at first glance but becomes crucial in the right context.

> *"Power is not given. Power is taken."*
> *— Anonymous*

Leverage is the fulcrum upon which every successful negotiation rests. The party with the most leverage controls the negotiation, but leverage is often misunderstood. Leverage is not about dominance; it's about understanding what the other party needs more than what you need. The art of negotiation lies in recognizing, enhancing, and using your leverage effectively.

Identifying Hidden Leverage

Leverage comes in many forms—time, resources, relationships, information. Often, what you consider insignificant can be a powerful tool in the negotiation. For example, if you control the timeline of the deal, you have leverage. If you have information the other party doesn't, you have leverage.

Creating Perceived Value

It is not just about what you bring to the table, but how you present it. Sometimes the perceived value of what you offer is more important than the actual value. By emphasizing the scarcity, uniqueness, or future benefits of your offer, you can enhance your leverage dramatically.

Actionable Takeaway

Always ask yourself: What does the other party need that I control? Enhance and leverage that value throughout the negotiation.

- Identify and amplify your leverage.
- Understand what the other party values most.
- Ensure your leverage is central to the negotiation.

Application

a. In a salary negotiation, the employee's leverage could be the unique skill set they bring, the strategic timing of their request, or the company's urgent need to retain top talent.

b. In a negotiation between a supplier and a retailer, the supplier realizes that they control not just the product, but the delivery schedule. The retailer needs the product urgently to meet a holiday rush. By highlighting their ability to meet the deadline (something the retailer's competitors cannot), the supplier increases their leverage, allowing them to negotiate better payment terms.

CHAPTER 4

The Law of Silence: Speak Only to Gain

In the silence, power is born. Resist the urge to fill every void with words. Often, silence forces the other party to reveal their hand or concede points. When you do speak, ensure your words add value. Every word must be a calculated move, every silence, a potential gain. Silence is one of the most underused tools in negotiation, but it's one of the most powerful.

People are uncomfortable with silence, and often rush to fill it with words—sometimes even words that weaken their position. Silence forces the other party to reveal more than they intended or reconsider their stance. A well-timed pause can lead to better offers or unexpected concessions. Silence is not passive; it's an active strategy that shifts the balance of power.

"Silence is one of the great arts of conversation." — Marcus Tullius Cicero

Silence is a weapon. It creates space for reflection, builds tension, and often forces the other party to fill the void. In negotiation, silence can be more powerful than any argument you make. Too many negotiators fear silence, rushing to fill it with concessions or unnecessary explanations, but in reality, silence often reveals more about the other party's position than any direct question.

The Power of Pausing

After making a proposal, resist the urge to immediately follow up with justifications or revisions. A well-timed pause often forces the other party to respond, filling the silence with valuable information or even unexpected concessions.

Reading the Room

Silence also allows you to observe body language and facial expressions. It gives you insight into what the other party is thinking, providing valuable data you can use to adjust your strategy.

Actionable Takeaway

Practice using silence in your everyday interactions. Ask a question and wait. Let the silence do the work. In negotiation, silence speaks louder than words.

- Resist the urge to fill every silence with conversation.
- Use silence to encourage the other party to offer more information.
- Let the silence pressurize the other party into making concessions.

Application

a. In a salary negotiation, after stating your desired compensation, resist the temptation to justify it immediately. Let the silence linger. Often, the employer will speak first, perhaps even offering more than you expected simply to fill the silence.

b. In a car dealership, after presenting your offer, remaining silent forces the salesperson to consider whether they can offer a better deal, knowing that you may be willing to walk away.

CHAPTER 5

The Law of Flexibility: Adapt, Don't Yield

Rigidity is the enemy of success in negotiation. While knowing your bottom line is essential, the path to it must be fluid. Adapt to changing circumstances without losing sight of your goals. Flexibility allows you to explore creative solutions, finding unexpected paths to victory while keeping your core interests intact. Rigid negotiators rarely win. Adaptable ones do.

Negotiation is fluid, and while you must remain clear on your ultimate goals, the path to reaching them should be flexible. Flexibility allows you to explore alternative solutions, unexpected alliances, and creative terms. Stubbornness can close doors, while adaptability opens new avenues to success. Being flexible doesn't mean being weak; it means keeping your options open and adjusting your strategy as the situation evolves.

> *"The measure of intelligence is the ability to change."* — Albert Einstein

Flexibility is the hallmark of a skilled negotiator. While knowing your goals is essential, achieving them requires adaptability. Rigidity can kill negotiations, whereas flexibility allows you to navigate roadblocks and find creative solutions that others might miss. Flexibility is not about giving in—it's about finding new ways to achieve your objectives.

Strategic Flexibility

Being flexible doesn't mean compromising on your core goals. It means being willing to adjust the path to those goals. The most effective negotiators know when to pivot without losing sight of the final objective. This can involve exploring alternative options, proposing different terms, or even reframing the negotiation entirely.

Non-Monetary Concessions

Often, flexibility in negotiation doesn't have to involve financial concessions. You can offer flexible timelines, additional services, or unique terms that satisfy the other party without reducing your own gain.

Actionable Takeaway

List alternative pathways to success before entering the negotiation. Think beyond monetary value. What other terms or concessions can you offer that would be seen as valuable?

- Be willing to shift tactics if your initial approach isn't working.
- Stay open to creative solutions or compromises.
- Know your non-negotiables but be flexible on how you get there.

Application

a. A tech company in a licensing negotiation for new software adapts their strategy by offering the client a revenue-sharing model instead of a flat fee, leading to a deal that benefits both parties.

b. A software company negotiating a licensing deal finds that the client is balking at the high upfront cost. Instead of lowering the price, the company offers a flexible payment plan spread over several years, along with additional training support. The client agrees, and the company maintains the original price while satisfying the client's budget concerns.

CHAPTER 6

The Law of Patience: Pressure Builds Over Time

Negotiation is rarely won in haste. Patience can outmanoeuvre urgency, allowing you to create pressure over time. The party that pushes too quickly often sacrifices too much. Wait for the right moment to strike, and never let your eagerness be a disadvantage.

> *"Patience is bitter, but its fruit is sweet."* —Jean-Jacques Rousseau

Time is your silent ally. Rushed negotiations are rarely successful. Time can be your greatest ally. Patience is the hidden force behind many successful negotiations. Rushing often leads to settling for less, while patience allows the other party's urgency to work in your favour. The party that feels the most pressure will often make concessions first. By being patient, you can wear down resistance and create the conditions where the other side is more willing to meet your terms.

In negotiation, time is a critical asset. The party that feels more time pressure is usually the one that makes more concessions. Patience allows you to let that pressure build on the other party while you remain composed. Hasty decisions lead to regret, whereas patience often forces the other side to blink first.

Time as a Weapon

The ability to wait creates psychological pressure. When the other party is in a rush to close a deal, they are more likely to make mistakes or offer concessions simply to move things forward. The ability to outwait your counterpart is a significant advantage.

Reading the Clock

Patience doesn't mean waiting indefinitely. It means understanding the timeline of the negotiation and strategically using delays to your advantage. You must know when to hold and when to press forward based on the dynamics of the conversation and external pressures.

Actionable Takeaway

When negotiating, consciously control the pace. Use time to let pressure work in your favour, and don't let the urgency of others push you into premature decisions.

- Be willing to wait, even when the other party is pressing for a quick decision.
- Recognize that urgency often signals opportunity for leverage.
- Use time to allow the other party's position to weaken.

In a property deal, the buyer waits for the seller to lower their price as the market cools and their property sits unsold. Patience results in a better deal.

Application

In a business acquisition, the buyer knows the seller is under pressure to close the deal quickly due to financial difficulties. By patiently waiting and not immediately accepting the seller's price, the buyer allows the pressure to build. Eventually, the seller lowers the price to close the deal faster.

CHAPTER 7
The Law of Reciprocity: Give to Get

A concession is not a loss if it's given to gain. This law teaches that strategic generosity builds trust and encourages reciprocation. By giving small, calculated concessions, you create a sense of obligation in the other party, paving the way for bigger gains down the line.

> *"You can have everything in life you want, if you will just help other people get what they want."*
> *— Zig Ziglar*

Negotiation is not about taking everything; it's about strategic exchange. When you give something of value, you create an expectation of reciprocity. Concessions can create goodwill and momentum toward a favorable outcome. But the key is making small, calculated concessions that encourage the other party to reciprocate with something of equal or greater value. The principle of reciprocity plays into the human desire for fairness. Always remember: the art of negotiation thrives on balance.

The principle of reciprocity governs human interactions. In negotiation, this law is about creating a sense of fairness and obligation. By offering something—whether it's a concession, a gesture, or even goodwill—you create an expectation that the other party will return the favour. But this law goes beyond simply trading concessions; it's about building rapport and trust that pave the way for larger gains.

Strategic Concessions

Offering concessions at the right time can shift the balance of the negotiation. By giving something small, you encourage the other party to respond with something of equal or greater value. But the key is to make these concessions appear more generous than they are.

Building Trust

Reciprocity builds relationships. In negotiations where future dealings are likely, giving creates goodwill and establishes trust. This lays the groundwork for future collaborations or negotiations where trust can be leveraged to your advantage.

Actionable Takeaway

Identify small, strategic concessions you can offer that create a sense of reciprocity without giving away your leverage. Make these concessions visible and frame them as generous.

- Offer small, strategic concessions to build trust.
- Frame your concessions as generous to encourage reciprocation.
- Ensure every concession is purposeful and leads to a greater gain.

Application

a. In a joint venture negotiation, one company offers to handle all the legal fees upfront. This generous gesture builds goodwill and leads the other party to agree to more favourable terms on revenue sharing.

b. In a business partnership negotiation, offering to cover legal fees upfront might encourage the other party to agree to more favourable profit-sharing terms down the line.

CHAPTER 8.

The Law of the Walkaway: Never Negotiate Without the Power to Leave

In negotiation, your power comes from the ability to walk away from a deal. When the other party knows you are not dependent on their agreement, the balance of power shifts dramatically in your favuor. The party who needs the deal less usually wins. This is why having a strong **BATNA** (Best Alternative to a Negotiated Agreement) is essential. Your walkaway point not only protects you from making bad deals but also gives you the confidence to push for better terms.

> "The most dangerous negotiation is the one you cannot walk away from."
> — Christopher Voss

The moment you feel you cannot walk away is the moment you lose. Always negotiate with an alternative or "Plan B" in your pocket. The ability to leave the table empowers you to hold firm on critical points and weakens your opponent's resolve. Fear of losing makes one reckless; strength lies in being able to walk.

Walking away from a deal gives you leverage that few can resist. When the other party knows you are not dependent on the outcome, they lose the power to pressure you into unfavourable terms. Always have a plan in place, whether it's an alternative deal or no deal at all. This mindset allows you to negotiate from a position of strength.

Understanding BATNA: Your BATNA is the best outcome you

can achieve if the current negotiation fails. The stronger your alternatives, the less pressure you feel to accept a suboptimal deal. A common mistake in negotiation is becoming too emotionally or financially invested in one outcome without considering alternatives.

Psychological Strength: Walking away shows strength. It signals that you value your own position enough not to settle for less. This can often force the other party to reconsider their demands and offer better terms out of fear of losing the deal entirely.

Actionable Takeaway

> ➢ Before entering any negotiation, clearly define your walkaway point and know your alternatives.
> ➢ Practice mentally detaching from the outcome so you don't feel desperate. Your willingness to walk away can be your most powerful leverage.

Application

A company negotiating a merger knows they have another interested buyer waiting. This gives them the power to reject offers that don't meet their terms, pushing the first party to offer a better deal, knowing the company can walk away without major losses.

Action Steps:

> ➢ Develop alternatives before entering the negotiation.
> ➢ Be clear on your non-negotiables and walk away if they aren't met.
> ➢ Always negotiate with the mindset that no deal is better than a bad deal.

A job candidate negotiating salary is able to walk away from a low offer because they have multiple job offers on the table. The employer, knowing this, increases the offer to match market value.

CHAPTER 9.

The Law of Emotional Control: Emotion Clouds Judgment

Negotiation is a psychological game. While emotions are natural, letting them control your behavior during negotiation can lead to poor decisions. The moment you allow anger, frustration, or desperation to guide your actions, you lose objectivity. Emotional intelligence is a crucial skill that allows you to manage both your own emotions and those of the other party, ensuring you stay rational and in control.

> *"He who is not everyday conquering some fear has not learned the secret of life."* — Ralph Waldo Emerson

Emotions, unchecked, are the enemy of reason. Never let frustration, excitement, or fear dictate your actions. Stay calm, calculated, and composed, no matter what is said or done. The one who controls their emotions controls the negotiation, for emotion in your opponent is often an opening to exploit.

The Trap of Anger

Anger can make you feel more powerful in the moment, but it clouds judgment and narrows your options. When you're emotional, you're more likely to overlook important details or make rash decisions that you regret later.

Controlling the Narrative

When the other party becomes emotional, use it to your

advantage. Stay calm and composed, and you will appear stronger and more in control. Emotional outbursts from the other side can reveal insecurities or vulnerabilities that you can leverage.

Emotional Intelligence (EQ)

High emotional intelligence allows you to read the other party's emotions, helping you navigate tricky conversations and prevent unnecessary conflict. The ability to manage both your own and others' emotions is key to building rapport and trust.

Emotions, especially negative ones like anger or frustration, cloud judgment and lead to poor decisions. Successful negotiators stay calm and composed, no matter how heated the discussion becomes. By controlling your emotions, you remain rational and focused on your goals. Moreover, when you keep your cool, you can use the emotions of the other party to your advantage.

Actionable Takeaway:

Practice mindfulness and emotional awareness. When tensions rise, focus on your breathing, stay composed, and stick to your strategy. Use the other party's emotional responses as clues to their underlying motivations or pressure points.

- Stay calm and composed, even when provoked.
- Use the emotional reactions of the other party to gauge their priorities.
- Focus on facts, not feelings, to keep the negotiation on track.

Application

a. In a high-stakes business negotiation, one side becomes visibly agitated and defensive. The other party remains calm and composed, making strategic offers and counteroffers. Eventually, the emotional side makes hasty concessions just to end the tension, allowing the calm side to secure a more favourable deal.

b. In a heated contract negotiation, one party becomes visibly frustrated, while the other remains calm. The calm party uses the frustration as leverage, knowing the frustrated side is likely to make hasty concessions to end the discussion.

CHAPTER 10

The Law of Framing: Control the Narrative, Control the Outcome

Framing is the psychological art of shaping how the negotiation is perceived. By controlling the narrative, you control the terms of the conversation. How you present your offer or position can completely change the other party's perception of value, fairness, and potential outcomes. Mastering the art of framing allows you to guide the negotiation toward your desired outcome, even when the facts don't change.

"It's not what you say, but how you say it." — George Bernard Shaw

Reframing Objections

When the other party raises an objection, don't respond defensively. Instead, reframe it in a way that turns it into a positive. For example, if someone says, "Your price is too high," you can reframe by saying, "That's because our product is built to last longer and requires less maintenance, saving you money over time."

Anchoring the Conversation

The first offer in any negotiation sets an anchor. By making the first offer, you establish a reference point around which the negotiation revolves. Even if the final outcome is somewhere in the middle, anchoring high or low can greatly influence the result.

Highlighting Value

Frame your proposal in terms of the benefits it brings to the other party, rather than focusing on cost. Instead of saying, "This is how much it costs," you can say, "This is how much value or savings you'll gain."

He who sets the frame controls the negotiation. Framing is the art of defining how the negotiation is perceived by both parties. It shapes expectations, parameters, and the perceived fairness of the outcome. By setting the frame, you direct the conversation toward your desired outcome. Reframing is equally powerful—it allows you to shift a conversation that's headed in the wrong direction back into more favorable territory.

> "It's not what you say, but how you say it." — George Bernard Shaw

By defining the terms, boundaries, and expectations of the discussion, you guide the other party into seeing the situation through your lens. Establish the frame early, and consistently reinforce it to shape the negotiation toward your desired result.

Framing is the psychological art of shaping how the negotiation is perceived. By controlling the narrative, you control the terms of the conversation. How you present your offer or position can completely change the other party's perception of value, fairness, and potential outcomes. Mastering the art of framing allows you to guide the negotiation toward your desired outcome, even when the facts don't change.

Anchoring the Conversation

The first offer in any negotiation sets an anchor. By making the first offer, you establish a reference point around which the negotiation revolves. Even if the final outcome is somewhere in the middle, anchoring high or low can greatly influence the result.

Highlighting Value

Frame your proposal in terms of the benefits it brings to the other party, rather than focusing on cost. Instead of saying, "This is how much it costs," you can say, "This is how much value or savings you'll gain."

Actionable Takeaway:

Always consider how you present your offers and responses. Practice reframing objections and questions in a way that reinforces your position. Control the narrative, and you will often control the outcome.

Actionable Takeaway

Always consider how you present your offers and responses. Practice reframing objections and questions in a way that reinforces your position. Control the narrative, and you will often control the outcome.

> - Set the tone and boundaries of the negotiation early.
> - Use language that reinforces your goals and positions.
> - Reframe any negative situations to reflect positively on your offer.

Application

 a. A contractor bids high on a project but frames it by emphasizing the quality of materials and long-term durability. Instead of focusing on the higher upfront cost, they focus on how much money the client will save in future repairs. The client agrees to the higher price because of the perceived long-term value.

 b. Reframing Objections: When the other party raises an objection, don't respond defensively. Instead, reframe it in a way that turns it into a positive. For example, if someone says, "Your price is too high," you can reframe by politely saying, "You are right, the reason is we know that A&A company values great standard and appreciate products built to last longer and requires less maintenance, saving you money over time."

c. In a pricing negotiation, the seller frames the higher price by emphasizing superior quality and long-term savings, shifting the focus from cost to value.

CHAPTER 11

The Law of Win-Win: Success Lies in Mutual Gain

A successful negotiation is not one where the other party is left broken or resentful. True mastery lies in crafting outcomes where both parties feel they have won. This ensures long-term relationships, repeat deals, and a reputation that precedes you. Negotiation is not war; it's a path to lasting, mutual benefit.

> *"You don't get what you deserve. You get what you negotiate."* — Chester Karrass

The best negotiations are those where both parties walk away feeling like they've won. This isn't just about being nice—it's about ensuring the long-term success of relationships. When both sides gain something valuable, they are more likely to follow through on the agreement and build future opportunities together. A win-win mindset ensures that neither party feels cheated, leading to a more sustainable and productive outcome.

Building Trust

Win-win negotiations build trust and rapport, making future deals easier. If the other party feels they've been treated fairly, they'll be more willing to work with you again.

Identifying Mutual Interests

Finding common ground is key to creating a win-win situation. This often involves looking beyond the surface to identify the deeper interests of both parties. What does the other side truly value, and how can you help them achieve it while securing what you want?

Creative Solutions

Sometimes, win-win outcomes are achieved through creativity. When traditional options don't seem to satisfy both sides, think outside the box. Explore non-monetary concessions, joint ventures, or staggered payments to meet everyone's needs.

Actionable Takeaway:

Approach negotiations with a win-win mindset by identifying what both sides value most. Be open to creative solutions that satisfy both parties' needs without sacrificing your core objectives.

- Look for solutions that benefit both sides.
- Focus on the long-term value of the relationship, not just the immediate outcome.
- Show empathy for the other party's needs, while maintaining your own goals.

Application

   a. In a partnership negotiation, both companies want control over the product's branding. Instead of one company conceding control, they agree to co-branding, where both logos appear on the product and each company takes responsibility for different aspects of marketing. Both companies walk away with shared ownership, ensuring a strong partnership and successful product launch.

   b. In a merger negotiation, both companies agree to

a shared leadership model, ensuring both retain influence and benefit from the combined resources.

CHAPTER 12
The Law of Persistence: 'No' Doesn't Mean Never

The word 'No' is often just the beginning of real negotiation. Persistence, tempered by patience, is the tool that turns initial rejections into opportunities. Every "no" should be seen as a challenge to uncover underlying needs, adjust strategies, or revisit the offer from a new angle.

"Most people give up just when they're about to achieve success."
— Ross Perot

Persistence separates winners from the rest.

The word "no!" is not the end of a negotiation—it's often just the beginning. Persistence means understanding that initial rejections are often part of the process. Keep refining your offer, probing for needs, and finding new ways to present your case. In many cases, persistence transforms initial resistance into eventual acceptance.

Rejection is part of the negotiation process, but the difference between average negotiators and great ones is persistence. Successful negotiators understand that "no" is often just a starting point for deeper discussions. They don't take rejection personally or as a final answer. Instead, they use it as a tool to probe for underlying concerns and adapt their approach.

Understanding Objections: A "no" is rarely final—it's an opportunity to learn more about what's truly holding the other party back. Often, objections are based on misunderstandings, incomplete information, or negotiable terms. Use rejection to ask clarifying questions and discover hidden needs or concerns.

The Power of Follow-Up: Persistence doesn't mean being pushy; it means staying engaged and patient. A well-timed follow-up can reopen the door that seemed closed. Negotiations often require multiple conversations, where each "no" brings you closer to a mutually acceptable "yes."

Handling Rejection with Grace: When faced with a "no," stay calm and poised. This signals to the other party that you're professional, and it keeps the door open for future discussions. Respect their current position but leave the possibility for a change open by saying, "I understand, but if things change, I'm always open to discussing it further."

Actionable Takeaway:

Don't take "no" at face value. View it as part of the negotiation process. Be persistent and use each rejection as a learning opportunity to refine your approach and uncover new opportunities.

- View "no" as a starting point, not the end.
- Keep the lines of communication open and continue refining your proposal.
- Use each rejection to uncover deeper insights about the other party's priorities.

Application

A software salesperson receives a "no" from a potential client due to budget concerns. Instead of giving up, the salesperson follows up a few months later with a new pricing model that fits the client's budget better. The client, impressed by the persistence and adaptability, agrees to a modified deal.

CHAPTER 13

The Law of Value Perception: Create and Communicate Value

Perception is often more powerful than reality in negotiation. The value you create is often shaped not just by what you offer, but by how it is perceived. Package your offer to reflect its worth. Sell the benefits, show the uniqueness, and highlight the risks the other party avoids by accepting it.

"Price is what you pay. Value is what you get." — Warren Buffett

In any negotiation, the perceived value of what you offer is often more important than its actual price. The way you present your product, service, or position can significantly influence the other party's perception of value. Often, negotiators focus too much on price, while overlooking the fact that people make decisions based on perceived value. By enhancing the perceived value of your offer, you can justify higher prices, better terms, or more favourable conditions.

Negotiation isn't just about pricing; it's about understanding how the other party perceives what you're offering. Whether you're negotiating a salary, a business deal, or a contract, your success hinges on your ability to communicate the value you bring to the table. The greater the value you can demonstrate, the more likely you are to close the deal on favourable terms.

Differentiating from Competitors

Your offer doesn't exist in a vacuum; the other party will often have other options. Your goal is to differentiate your offer by emphasizing its unique benefits and advantages. Highlight features, services, or aspects that make your offer stand out from others.

Building Emotional Value

People make decisions based on emotions as much as they do on logic. When negotiating, it's crucial to show not just the financial or practical benefits, but also how your offer will improve the other party's life or business. Whether it's reducing stress, simplifying processes, or enhancing reputation, emotional value can sometimes outweigh cost concerns.

Understanding the Other Side's Perception

One of the best ways to create value is to ask the right questions and understand what the other side values most. For some, time may be more important than money. For others, security, trust, or prestige may drive decisions. Tailoring your pitch to these specific needs can shift the negotiation in your favour.

Actionable Takeaway:

- Always highlight the unique value you bring to the negotiation, not just the price.
- Focus on how your offer will solve problems, meet needs, or deliver exceptional results for the other party.

By communicating value effectively, you shift the focus away from price and onto benefits.

Application

A high-end consultant is negotiating with a client who balks at their price. Instead of reducing the fee, the consultant frames their offer in terms of long-term business growth, emphasizing that while the upfront cost is higher, the return on investment over time will be significant due to their unique strategies that competitors can't offer. By shifting the client's focus from immediate costs to long-term gains, the consultant closes the deal without lowering their price.

CHAPTER 14

Bringing It All Together: Mastering the Laws

Now that we've walked through each of the 12 Immutable Laws of Negotiation, let's bring it all together. Success in negotiation comes from mastering a blend of psychology, strategy, and human understanding. While each law offers powerful individual insights, their true strength lies in their interplay.

To truly become a master negotiator, you need to:

1. Prepare Relentlessly (The Law of Preparation)—Never walk into a negotiation without fully understanding the landscape.

2. Leverage Power Effectively (The Law of Leverage)—Recognize your sources of power and strategically apply them to gain the upper hand.

3. Harness the Power of Silence (The Law of Silence)—Use pauses and silence to gather information and maintain control.

4. Remain Flexible (The Law of Flexibility)—Adapt your tactics to changing conditions while keeping your ultimate goal in focus.

5. Be Patient (The Law of Patience)—Allow pressure to build on the other party, and avoid rushing into decisions.

6. Create Reciprocity (The Law of Reciprocity)—Offer small concessions to build goodwill and encourage reciprocation.

7. Have the Power to Walk Away (The Law of the Walkaway)—Be willing to leave the table if necessary, and always know your

alternatives.

8. Control Your Emotions (The Law of Emotional Control)—Stay calm, focused, and in control of your emotional responses.

9. Frame the Negotiation (The Law of Framing)—Control how the terms of the negotiation are perceived to guide the outcome in your favour.

10. Seek Win-Win Solutions (The Law of Win-Win)—Build deals that provide value to both sides, ensuring long-term success.

11. Persist with Confidence (The Law of Persistence)—Never accept rejection as the final word; use it to probe deeper and push forward.

12. Communicate Value (The Law of Value Perception)—Present your offer in a way that maximizes its perceived value, making it irresistible to the other party.

Becoming a Master Negotiator

Negotiation is an art form that can transform your life and career. Whether you're negotiating a business deal, a salary raise, or even everyday situations like buying a car, the principles you've learned here will help you achieve more successful outcomes.

The key to mastering negotiation is constant practice. Start small—apply these laws in daily interactions and observe the results. As you build your skills, you'll begin to notice how much easier it becomes to create win-win situations, maintain control, and achieve your goals.

These laws, adhered to and mastered, pave the road to negotiation success. They transform a simple exchange of terms into a strategic, artful process where value is maximized, relationships are maintained, and your goals are achieved.

Remember that every negotiation is different, but these 12 laws will serve as a reliable framework to guide your approach. Over time, you'll refine your ability to read people, anticipate objections, and close deals that others might think impossible.

FINAL NOTE
Your Path to Mastery

Negotiation is more than just a skill; it's a gateway to achieving what matters most in life—whether it's financial success, personal satisfaction, or meaningful relationships. By mastering the 12 Immutable Laws of Negotiation, you have equipped yourself with a powerful framework for handling any situation that requires influence, persuasion, and strategy.

Throughout this book, you've learned that negotiation is not about manipulating or overpowering the other party. Instead, it's about finding solutions, building trust, and creating lasting value for everyone involved. Youve discovered that preparation, patience, and understanding human psychology are just as critical as the terms of the deal itself. These principles will serve as your guide in both simple everyday conversations and high-stakes, life-changing negotiations.

The Journey Does not End Here

Mastering negotiation is not a destination, but a continuous journey. The more you practice these laws, the more intuitive they will become. You'll begin to see negotiations in every aspect of your life, and with each new challenge, your ability to navigate the complexities of human interaction will deepen.

As you move forward, remember these key lessons:

Never underestimate the power of preparation: Walking into any negotiation without a clear understanding of your position, the other party's needs, and the broader context will put you at a disadvantage. Do your homework and know your leverage.

Stay flexible: No negotiation follows a straight path. Be ready to adapt and shift your strategy, but always keep your final goal in mind.

Silence is powerful: In a world full of noise, your ability to pause and listen can give you more control than speaking ever will.

Emotion is not your enemy: Learn to manage it—both your own and the other party's—to steer conversations in your favour.

The Legacy You Build Through Negotiation

Great negotiators do not just close deals—they build legacies. They create lasting partnerships, develop reputations of fairness and competence, and leave people wanting to work with them again and again. The tools you now possess will not only help you get what you want today but also set the foundation for long-term success and influence. The impact of mastering negotiation goes beyond contracts and agreements; it shapes your ability to lead, inspire, and create change in every area of your life.

Your Future as a Negotiator

As you close this book, I encourage you to make negotiation a conscious part of your everyday life. Challenge yourself to apply the laws in small situations—whether it's negotiating with a colleague, discussing a decision with family, or making a significant purchase. Notice how your mindset begins to shift, and how these principles help you stay calm, focused, and persuasive in every interaction.

Each negotiation you enter, no matter the stakes, is an opportunity to grow. With every conversation, you sharpen your skills. With every deal, you deepen your understanding of human behavior and influence.

The Power of Persistence

Mastering negotiation isn't about never failing; it's about persistence. There will be times when you don't get the outcome you expected. That's normal. What separates a great negotiator from an average one is the ability to learn from every experience and come back stronger. Each setback is an opportunity to refine your approach, sharpen your strategy, and continue evolving.

With time and practice, these laws will become second nature to you. You'll walk into negotiations with confidence, knowing that you have the tools to navigate any scenario. You'll be able to lead with empathy, listen with intention, and close deals with precision.

Practical Exercises to Sharpen Your Negotiation Skills

To take your negotiation skills to the next level, it's essential to put theory into practice. Here are a few exercises you can try:

    1. Scenario Practice: Create a list of hypothetical negotiation scenarios (e.g., negotiating for a new job, buying a house, closing a business deal). Practice with a partner, taking turns playing the roles of both sides. After each round, evaluate what worked and what didn't.

    2. Silence Exercise: In your next conversation, practice the Law of Silence. Ask a question or make a statement and pause. Count to 10 in your head before speaking again. Observe how silence shifts the dynamic.

    3. Framing Drill: Take a real-life situation where you didn't get the outcome you wanted and rewrite the conversation. Focus on reframing your responses to guide the conversation toward a more favorable result.

    4. Emotional Control Practice: In moments of tension or frustration (even outside of negotiation), focus on keeping your

emotions in check. Try to keep your voice calm and your body language neutral. This will help build emotional resilience for future negotiations.

Your Future is in Your Hands

You now hold the keys to unlocking the full potential of negotiation in your life. Whether you are negotiating for your business, your career, your relationships, or your personal goals, the skills you've gained here will help you achieve greater success, influence, and fulfilment.

As you move forward, remember that negotiation is not just about getting what you want—it's about creating value for everyone involved. When you approach negotiation with integrity, confidence, and a commitment to long-term success, you'll find that the possibilities are limitless.

The power of negotiation is now yours. Use it wisely, and let it shape your future in ways you never imagined possible.

To your success.

www.ingramcontent.com/pod-product-compliance
Lightning Source LLC
Chambersburg PA
CBHW030515220526
45464CB00006B/2800